WHY NOT?

why *not?*

How to Bring the
Liturgy About

TURLOUGH BAXTER

VERITAS

Published 2017 by
Veritas Publications
7–8 Lower Abbey Street
Dublin 1, Ireland

publications@veritas.ie
www.veritas.ie

ISBN 978 1 84730 762 0

10 9 8 7 6 5 4 3 2 1

A catalogue record for this book is available from the British
Library.

Designed by Lir Mac Cárthaigh
Printed in Ireland by Walsh Colour Print, Co. Kerry

*Veritas books are printed on paper made from the wood pulp of
managed forests. For every tree felled, at least one tree is planted,
thereby renewing natural resources.*

ACKNOWLEDGEMENTS

I would like to express my thanks to Maura, Pamela, Leeann, Daragh and Lir from Veritas for helping to bring this book to completion, to Fr Danny and Sr Moira from the National Centre for Liturgy for facilitating it, to Fr Tom from St Mel's Cathedral for the use of the images, to Fr Mark for his advice, and to my family and my friends Brendan and Damien for encouraging me to bring this book about.

Liturgical signs will be made meaningful
by the quantity of the water in the rite of
sprinkling and the density of the smoke in
the thurible. When signs are large enough
to be seen, loud enough to be heard, present
enough to be touched, aromatic enough
to be smelled, and delightful enough to be
tasted, they reveal their deeper layers of
meaning and enhance the prayers of the
faithful gathered.

Paul Turner,
Let Us Pray: A Guide to the
Rubrics of the Mass

Contents

Sometimes you have to state the obvious.
These 'Why Not?' suggestions are a
simple consideration of how best to bring
the goals of the *General Instruction on the
Roman Liturgy* (*GIRM*) to life; they are
what I call Incarnational Liturgy, or a way
to make these principles real and true to
the tradition, and the parish contexts in
which we work. Some can treat liturgies as
ritualist, but liturgy is more than that – it
is an expression of our communal faith and
an entry into the tradition that has been
handed down to us. The skill of the presider
is to make that tradition alive and real for
the Church in a particular time and place.

The role of the presider is key to holding
all these elements together, but that is

not to say that it is the priest's Mass and that we simply come as spectators. No, we are all partakers in the liturgy. Indeed, in many church renovations the placing of the baptismal font at the entrance is a constant reminder to us of this. Baptism is not something that we 'get', but what we become. We gather at the Sunday Eucharist or any liturgy because we are members of the baptised community in that place. Think of those words of the New Testament: 'You are a holy race, a royal priesthood, a holy nation.' We gather because this is our place and we have a right and duty to be there (*Sacramentum Caritatis*, 18).

Liturgy is a relationship; liturgy is a dialogue; it is never something that excludes us. Think of the dialogue before the preface of the *GIRM*; it is in its essence a conversation or call to us to do this work together with the priest. But we must also be careful. One of the major criticisms of the way liturgy is celebrated is that the liturgy is turned in on itself; in other words, Christ can end up being excluded and we simply do what we want, in the way we want. Liturgy is not about that. We gather as a community here, but also as a community of the Church down through the ages. Think of the litany of saints; it reminds us that what we do, we do in the context of a tradition that has been handed down to us, not so that we will be subservient to it, but so that we may find in it a treasure trove of wisdom, practice and belief that has made and sustained the people of God from age to age.

Liturgy, then, is prepared not planned. The liturgist is the artist who sees and releases the wonders of the liturgy for a worshipping people. They are never one to impose their view, but instead enable the true beauty to be seen. I have always loved the description of the artist as the person who sees with 'sight, insight and excite'. That also is the role of the good liturgist.

This collection is made up of nearly twelve years of snippets on liturgy that appeared in *Intercom* magazine from 2004–16. They were written as responses to what is outlined in the *General Instruction on the Roman Missal*, as well as a number of other resources. They appeared in no particular order in the magazine, but have been gathered here in this publication by category. These will first of all express general principles of the liturgy, then look at the Liturgy of the Eucharist and finally other elements including seasons and sacraments.

These are not meant to create a perfect celebration of the liturgy – we can never be perfect but we keep on trying. What I hope is that these will be of use for parish liturgy groups to reflect on and will help in the development of their Sunday Eucharist as an expression of what the liturgy tries to bring about. It is not an exhaustive list but a helpful guide.

The call of the *Constitution on the Liturgy* (*Sacramentum Caritatis*) from Vatican II is for noble simplicity. Let this message be seen for what it is. If our preoccupation in liturgy is solely with the elements and not with its purpose as a whole, we will end up fussing constantly about small things like what altar cloths to use. Liturgy is so much more than that. In presenting these points, I try to express the purpose and meaning behind them so as to get to the root of what we are trying to do.

The liturgy has developed through five dimensions: theological, historical, spiritual, pastoral and juridical. What has been handed down to us has been shaped in this way. As liturgists, we need to be sensitive to these and not just become one dimensional in our approach.

Liturgy has a style and form. Others have written style manuals to express this. Style can never be gained by just focussing on the externals, but by figuring out the core and heart of what it is about.

I hope this book will in some small way help to develop that point for liturgy groups in parishes today.

CHAPTER ONE

The Importance and Dignity of the Eucharistic Celebration

The celebration of Mass, as the action of Christ and the People of God arrayed hierarchically, is the centre of the whole Christian life for the Church both universal and local, as well as for each of the faithful individually. (GIRM, 16)

'Reading the Mass' is a phrase you still find people using to describe the way the priest presides at the celebration of the Eucharist. The liturgical books are to be used as aids to the liturgy and are not meant to dominate it or hide the eucharistic elements on the altar. In preparing for the Mass, attention is to be given not just to the scriptures but to all the variable texts provided.

Why not take care to place only these elements on the altar, so as to ensure that the vessels are visible to all assembled and clearly suggest one bread and one cup?

Silence is a facet of the Mass which sometimes makes us feel uncomfortable; however, its role is very important. The new *GIRM* tells us that silence should be observed 'so that all may dispose themselves to carry out the sacred action ... and meditate briefly on what they have heard'.

Why not introduce more space for silence, especially following each reading, by starting with a short period of silence and gradually letting it increase, so that the Word may have time to settle within us?

One of the striking features of the new translation of the Roman Missal is the constant reference to and quotation from the holy scriptures. We have long been using the scriptures for our reflection and meditation.

Why not also include the Missal as a place to find inspiration for prayer? In this way, we can make the Sunday Eucharist texts, not only the scriptural but also the variable prayers, the commons and propers, truly become the source and summit of our prayer life.

The introduction of the new translation of the Roman Missal represented much more than simply the alteration of the words we use. It marked a movement towards a stronger focus on the sacredness of the liturgy we celebrate. This focus is not only dependent on the words we use, but also on an awareness that each individual element has the possibility to highlight or diminish that sense of the sacred.

Why not ensure that the liturgical space, elements, vessels, vestments, music and manner in which the liturgy is executed highlights this sacredness?

The role of music in the liturgy is fundamental, not for an entertainment or decorative purpose, but to highlight the ritual, emphasise the sacred, unite the assembly and create a sense of dialogue with the presider. The *GIRM* mentions that, in choosing the pieces to be sung, 'preference should be given to those that are of greater importance and especially to those to be sung by the priest or the deacon or the lector with the people responding, or by the priest and people together' (40). This is greatly expressed in the dialogue at the start of the preface also.

Why not encourage the singing of this at each Eucharist, or at least on Sundays, to help achieve this musical role for presider and assembly?

The Eucharistic celebration is an action of Christ and the Church, namely, the holy people united and ordered under the Bishop. It therefore pertains to the whole Body of the Church, manifests it, and has its effect upon it. (*GIRM*, 91)

In light of this, we need to ask whom we might be excluding from fruitful participation in the liturgy; for example, those living with deafness. The National Chaplaincy to Deaf People offers a service whereby someone is made available to interpret at significant liturgies throughout the country.

Why not make contact with the National Chaplaincy to Deaf People and use this service to enable deaf members of the Body of Christ to participate more fully in the liturgy?

If we see the role of music in the liturgy as just a nice 'added extra', then we fail to see that it is truly essential. Music has always been at the heart of Christian worship. As the *GIRM* tells us, singing is a sign of the heart's joy. Music, then, is not just the role of a choir, important as their role is, but also of the priest and the people, in dialogue, responses, acclamations, etc.

Why not, as presider, get actively involved with the music – no matter your talent level – to highlight its central importance in enabling the faithful to more fully express their praise to God?

Quite often when people ask me for musical resources they follow up with the question: is it on CD? One big collection that is on CD is *Sing the Mass*, which is an anthology of Mass settings by Irish composers. This is available in Veritas. It is a resource that also reminds us of the wide variety of composers we have working in the country. Many of them have CDs out and some have recordings available on their websites.

Why not take this opportunity to look up the composers from the *Sing the Mass* collection on their websites and explore the many other pieces they have written.

Perhaps get your parish to invest in some of these collections and discover the immense talent of our Irish composers and the beauty of their compositions?

A teacher once said to me that 'faith is not taught, it's caught'. Maybe that is true of liturgy as well: the best tuition is found in good experiences. One such expression of this is the Irish Church Music Association Summer School held in Maynooth each July.

Why not recommend the event to those involved in music and liturgy in your parish as a way of discovering how beautiful our worship can be?

Symbolism lies at the heart of so much of the liturgy. Symbols are also used to try to express an element or focus of a season or feast; however, care needs to be taken that they do not take over from the primary symbols that lie at the heart of the liturgy: the altar, ambo, chair and cross.

Why not ensure that these primary symbols are always highlighted and enhanced rather than hidden, as they so often are, by other seasonal or devotional elements or decorations, which, while well-intentioned, can obscure what lies at the heart of each liturgy.

CHAPTER TWO

Gathering Rite

Christ is really present in the very liturgical assembly gathered in his name, in the person of the minister, in his word, and indeed substantially and continuously under the Eucharistic species. (GIRM, 27)

Those who, as the *GIRM* says, 'meet the faithful at the church entrance, lead them to appropriate places, and direct processions' fulfil a liturgical role (105). Throughout the summer months especially, we should be aware that many people who are staying in our area only briefly might like to join us for the Eucharist on Sunday.

Why not ensure that the times of Masses and all other liturgical events in the parish are clearly displayed in the church entry area and that those who join on Sunday are made to feel welcome and included?

The eucharistic celebration is an action of Christ and the Church. The *GIRM* tells us that there should be no appearance of individualism or division within the celebration. This is expressed by singing, posture and the church layout.

Why not emphasise to those who lead the music at the liturgy the important role of the entrance antiphon or hymn in promoting a sense of unity between all those participating in the celebration of the Eucharist?

The *GIRM* discusses the gestures and bodily posture that we use in the liturgy. These are to be conducive to making the entire celebration 'resplendent with beauty and noble simplicity' (42). Common postures and gestures can also be used as markers of solidarity and unity between the members of the Christian community gathered together.

Why not ensure that postures and gestures are held in common, not only within individual parish communities but also between parishes, so as to highlight the commonality of our activities, and to avoid being guided simply by 'private inclinations or arbitrary choice'?

A processional route through the assembly at the start of our liturgies may seem overly formal to some; however, a short sacristy-

to-altar walk can often portray ministers
as actors on a stage, separate from those
gathered. A processional route through
the assembly serves the very significant
function of connecting the presider with
the faithful and gathering everyone into the
celebration in a spirit of togetherness.

Why not ensure that the natural
processional route for all ministers passes
through the assembly? This will enable
all to fully – consciously and actively –
participate in the liturgy.

The use of incense can be seen by some
as lavish or only associated with funerals,
but *GIRM* 75 emphasises that its use
is important in symbolising our prayer
ascending to the Lord and states that
both the priest and the people should be

'incensed' by virtue of their sacred ministry and baptismal dignity respectively.

Why not invest in good quality incense that offers a more attractive fragrance and after the gifts incense the faithful to reinforce for them the dignity of who they are and the inclusiveness of their role in the eucharistic liturgy?

The presider's chair at the liturgy is for more than just practical use. It is symbolic of the role of the priest as the one who presides over the praying faithful. It should be clearly visible to those assembled and placed in a position that allows the presider to easily relate to the people.

Why not, if this has not already been the practice, use the chair as the place from which the Introductory Rites and the

Prayer of the Faithful are lead, as specified in the *GIRM*? This, in turn, will highlight the function of the altar as the place we approach for the Liturgy of the Eucharist and the ambo as the place of the Word.

The liturgy in its essence is a dialogue. In practice, this dialogue is between the presider and assembly. Some of those who preside at liturgy can have a tendency to pre-empt the responses of the assembly, for example also saying 'Amen' to the opening sign of the cross or instantly replying to the 'Lord have mercy'.

Why not ensure that, as the presider, we give time to let people respond as an assembly, thereby developing the sense of dialogue with our Lord that comes through the presider's mediation?

What in past times was called the opening
prayer now has the title of Collect, for
that better expresses what it is. More than
just a few lines of text, the Collect is in
itself a dialogue. It begins with the priest
addressing and looking at the people, then
gives the space for the people to collect the
things for which they wish to pray in this
Eucharist; then the priest raises his hands in
prayer, spoken in the name of all present, to
which the people respond 'Amen'.

Why not spend more time in preparation of
the Collect and the two other presidential
prayers so that this formula of prayer –
naming God, recounting divine attributes
and deeds, petition and conclusion – may
become a pattern for all of our prayer lives?

We all know about the desire for periods of silence during the liturgy; however, there can be a fine line between prayerful meditation and people simply wondering if someone has missed their cue.

Why not hold a period of silence before the Liturgy of the Word, as suggested in the *GIRM*? Even a short period might heighten people's expectations of the Word that is to come.

Aidan Kavanagh in his book on liturgical style, *Elements of Rite*, talks of the liturgical minister as serving the assembly. He tells us that they 'preside not over the assembly but within it'. For this they need to know both assembly and liturgy well.

Why not let the liturgical ministers process through the assembly and not just come out from a sacristy doorway for our celebration of Mass, expecially for the Sunday Eucharist? This may help to gather as one all who have attended and remind the ministers of those that they have come to serve.

Musicam Sacram talks of the most important elements of the liturgy that are to be sung. It states that acclamations and responses between priest and people are the most important. Even if recited, these responses play an important role in allowing the assembly to participate in the celebration of the liturgy. Those who preside should respect the role of the faithful and ensure that they do not undermine its significance.

Why not take care that the importance of these interactions is respected and that the turning of pages in the Missal, or other distractions, does not undermine them?

CHAPTER THREE

Liturgy of the Word

*By their silence and singing the people make
God's word their own, and they also affirm
their adherence to it by means of the Profession
of Faith. Finally, having been nourished by it,
they pour out their petitions in the Prayer of the
Faithful for the needs of the entire Church and
for the salvation of the whole world.* (*GIRM*,
55)

The ambo is to be a place of dignity
worthy of the Word of God. From the
ambo, the *GIRM* tells us, only the readings,
the Responsorial Psalm and the Easter
proclamation are to be proclaimed. It may
be used also for giving the homily and for
announcing the intentions of the Prayer
of the Faithful. We would not use the altar
for anything other than that for which it is
intended; it is the same with the ambo.

Why not decide on some other suitable position for cantor or commentator to stand at the appropriate times, rather than at the ambo?

Lent is a good time to focus on the Word of God. The emphasis is not just on understanding or listening to that word, but hearing it deeply in our lives. At liturgy, the lector has an important role in allowing that be achieved.

Why not, as one action to highlight this period, help all who read to focus not only on being people who tell a story, but also on being ministers who give over their voices so that God can speak through them, thus enabling the listener to truly hear the voice of God in their lives?

It is preferable that the responsorial Psalm be sung, at least as far as the people's response is concerned... If the Psalm cannot be sung, then it should be recited in such a way that it is particularly suited to foster meditation on the word of God. (**GIRM**, 61)

Why not highlight, especially with ministers of the Word, the important role of the psalm as a meditation? Why not suggest that it be proclaimed in a different style and tone to the other scriptural texts, so as to engage the congregation's response?

Once at a commemoration ceremony I noticed a line in the booklet that read, 'This booklet contains sacred text; please dispose of with care.' Shortly afterwards I was walking by a church with soiled missalettes discarded on the ground outside. With the common use of missalettes, we should be careful not to suggest that what they contain is disposable.

Why not make an effort to ensure that the congregation appreciates not only the words of the liturgy but the very pages they are printed on? This way we are reminded always of the sacredness of the text.

The Liturgy of the Word is an important form of communication. Those who minister the Word are not speaking their own word but giving their voice to let God be heard.

Why not take some time each year to work with your readers on their oration skills, so ensuring that the Word can be clearly heard?

The psalms are prayers that have been used and shaped by generations of believers over thousands of years. In our celebration of the Eucharist they are mostly only used for the Responsorial Psalm. Quite often this can be replaced by pieces of music that might be related to the scripture of that day. The desire might be to use an attractive piece of music but the sentiments of the text can get lost.

Why not ensure that a greater focus is placed on the psalms, whether sung or recited, so as to help all who take part in the liturgy to come to see them, like their forebears, as the rich prayers that they are? Indeed, the use of the psalms is also appropriate for the entrance and communion antiphons.

In liturgy, silence is not meant to be an embarrassing, barren or uncontrolled lack of sound that occurs because things have broken down or no one knows what to do next, but rather a purposeful period when people communicate in a way that is deeper than words.

Why not try to develop in our celebration of the liturgy a calmness that provides silence after the readings, after the homily and during communion, so that the power of God's presence may be sensed in the unique experience of people gathered and being still in silence together?

Autumn can be the time when a lot of planning for the new liturgical year takes place. With schools reopened, a number of elements of the liturgy can also be reviewed; choirs restart after the summer break and new readers are recruited. It is also a good time to set goals for the liturgy. The role of the psalm continues to be an area that needs to be addressed. The *GIRM* states that 'it is unlawful to substitute other, non-biblical texts for the readings and responsorial psalm, which contain the Word of God' (57).

Why not make it a priority this year to get those involved in music to take on a number of psalm settings from the common psalms for each season? These can be found in the lectionary. By doing this, the continuing tendency to substitute the psalms with non-biblical texts may be reduced.

The *GIRM* tells us that the Alleluia or verse before the gospel reading may be omitted if they are not sung. By implication, the acclamation is best expressed when

accompanied by music. Those who recite
the gospel acclamation quickly discover they
have diminished its power as a greeting to
the Lord.

Why not ensure that it is sung at all
liturgical celebrations so as to enable
those who take part to attune their ears
to the significance of hearing the gospel
proclaimed?

For centuries the custom of having the
Book of the Gospels present on the altar
has been an important element of liturgical
celebrations. The Book of the Gospels is
an icon of Christ, as it speaks directly of
Our Lord. In the entrance procession, this
book symbolises the Lord who gathers
us together to hear his word; in the exit
procession, it guides the way we are called
to live our lives.

Why not use the Book of the Gospels, or if you do not have one, acquire one, so that this ancient custom may be maintained in the liturgy?

The *GIRM* tells us about the Alleluia: 'An acclamation of this kind constitutes a rite or act in itself, by which the gathering of the faithful welcomes and greets the Lord who is about to speak to them in the Gospel and profess their faith by means of the chant' (62).

Why not sing the Alleluia every day (except during Lent) as a way to highlight its importance, but also as a way to integrate music into the liturgy and encourage congregational singing? It needs no words or complicated melody to achieve this. Using it every day will highlight the importance of music as something more than just an added extra.

In our celebration of the Eucharist, the proclamation of the Creed can often be rushed or made on 'autopilot'. Familiarity with the text can mean we do not fully engage with what we are saying.

Why not try to highlight the Creed by singing it, or at least part of it? There is a very good tone for the Apostles' Creed by John O'Keeffe in *Sing the Mass* (Dublin: Veritas Publications, 2011). Alternatively, the Lourdes chant – 'Credo, Credo, Credo, Amen' – could be used to introduce and conclude the Creed. This will help focus attention on the Creed in a new way and allow us to hear what we are called to profess with our hearts.

In the Prayer of the Faithful, the people respond in a certain way to the word of God which they have welcomed in faith and, exercising the office of their baptismal priesthood, offer prayers to God for the salvation of all. (GIRM, 69)

Why not develop a group in the parish who gather to pray with the Word of God during the week in preparation for the Sunday Eucharist, taking on the ministry of preparing this form of prayer for the parish Sunday Mass? They will need training to develop a way of being able to express these prayers, as the *GIRM* also reminds us, 'in a few words'.

CHAPTER FOUR

Liturgy of the Eucharist

For Christ took the bread and the chalice and gave thanks; he broke the bread and gave it to his disciples, saying, 'Take, eat, and drink: this is my Body; this is the cup of my Blood. Do this in memory of me.' Accordingly, the Church has arranged the entire celebration of the Liturgy of the Eucharist in parts corresponding to precisely these words and actions of Christ. (GIRM, 72)

The altar is so much more than the shelf or storage place that it can end up being in some churches. It is the symbol of the Lord's presence, which we gather around at each liturgy.

Why not, if there are no servers available, ask the ministers of holy communion to help prepare the altar at the offertory time rather than have the gifts and other elements placed there from the beginning? This will help to preserve the integrity of the altar's role in the liturgy and better express how we as a community gather around it for the Eucharist.

I have faced both sides in the incense debate. There are those who have criticised me for using it and those who have criticised me for not using it. The *GIRM* tells us that it is used 'so as to signify the Church's offering and prayer rising like incense in the sight of God'. It gives us another dimension in the liturgy, but needs to be used with sensitivity.

Why not use high quality incense and a clean thurible each time, perhaps with tinfoil so that any old residue can be removed?

The *GIRM* tells us that it is preferable for the faithful, like the priest, to receive the Lord's Body from hosts consecrated at the same Mass, so that 'even by means of the signs Communion will stand out more clearly as a participation in the sacrifice actually being celebrated' (85).

Why not calculate the exact amount required rather than filling the ciborium to the top for fear of running short of hosts? This will reduce the chances of a large quantity being left over to be consumed later. In this way, we will more fully express the meaning of *GIRM* 85.

Sometimes familiarity can breed contempt. In the liturgy, our ears can become so used to hearing a certain prayer over and over

again that the meaning can be lost. While
Eucharistic Prayers II & III are most often
used, there are, in total, ten Eucharistic
Prayers approved for use within the liturgy.

Why not search these out and prepare them
so that, when used in the proper context,
they can well express what we celebrate at
Mass?

In all of our liturgies, especially in the
celebration of the Eucharist, we gather
around the altar as a symbol of the Lord,
the Head of the Body, the Church. The altar
is not just a convenient place to celebrate
the Eucharist, or a resting place for the
materials of the Mass; it is much more.

Why not let the presentation of gifts be a
greater expression of the preparation and
dressing of the altar with corporal, book,

vessels, bread and wine? None of these should be in place until the appropriate time.

Paul Turner, in his book *Let Us Pray*, tells us that the practice of the priest placing one large host on a paten separate from the vessel from which everyone else would receive, is a tradition that developed when the faithful did not receive communion at Mass, or, if they did, they were given communion from a ciborium in the tabernacle. This practice weakens the symbolism of the Eucharist as a sacrament of unity.

Why not include the host from which the priest will receive (which, according to *GIRM* 321, is to be large enough to be broken into several portions) in a more

paten-like ciborium, to better express one
bread, one body?

The prophet Elijah discovered the Lord in
the gentle breeze and not in the earthquake,
wind or fire (1 Kgs 19:11–14).

Why not remember, during all our liturgies,
the importance of sacred silence in allowing
the Lord to speak to us as he did Elijah?

Each gesture within the liturgy should
appropriately express the meaning of each
element: standing for the gospel reading
suggests attentiveness to the Word;
kneeling for the consecration acknowledges
respect and reverence; sitting for the
homily allows us to be attentive to what is
being said. The increasing tendency to sit

for the consecration misses the meaning completely, suggesting that those assembled are simply spectators rather than partakers.

Why not encourage those who are assembled to stand, if they can at all, so as to show that we are all participants in this eucharistic celebration? Why not also use this posture for the gathering and dismissal as laid out in the *GIRM*?

The dialogue that introduces the preface to the Eucharistic Prayer is of great importance. In its invitation and response it expresses the desire to unite the congregation with the priest, who addresses the prayer to God in their name.

Furthermore, the meaning of the Prayer is that the entire congregation of the faithful should

*join itself with Christ in confessing the great
deeds of God and in the offering of Sacrifice.*
(*GIRM*, 78)

Why not highlight this element by
singing the dialogue and encouraging the
congregation to respond to this simple and
well-known tone? A sung dialogue does
not necessarily imply that the preface must
be sung, but it would give definition to the
beginning of the Eucharistic Prayer, as
the doxology and Amen give to the end,
and strengthen the role of the other sung
acclamations that follow.

The Eucharistic Prayer, while led by the
one who presides at the liturgy, is still a
prayer of the whole assembly. (Notice the
number of times that the word 'we' is used.)
This unity is expressed by participation in
responses and acclamations that build up a

dialogue. It is important that the musical settings that are chosen for these elements should be from the same source; and for all to take their part it is important that this be accessible and frequently used.

Why not work with all involved in music ministry to agree on one setting for the eucharistic acclamations that can be used at all Masses in the parish, so that everybody can develop the habit of taking their part, as they should?

One of the earliest titles for the celebration of the Eucharist was 'The Breaking of Bread'. The *GIRM* tells us that the eucharistic bread should be made in such a way that the priest at Mass is able to break it into parts for distribution to at least some of the faithful. This will highlight both the unity of all in the one bread, and the sign

of charity in its distribution among the
brothers and sisters.

Why not ensure that the principal host
consecrated at Mass is not consumed solely
by the celebrant, but is instead broken
so that at least some members of the
congregation will be able to share it?

The sign of peace is an important part of
the celebration of the Eucharist. In a time
of fear and conflict, it offers us the challenge
and hope of peace and points us to the One
who is 'our peace'. Some churches highlight
this by singing a peace hymn during this
gesture. *Sacramentum Caritatis* calls for
greater restraint at this time: '[N]othing
is lost when the sign of peace is marked by
sobriety which preserves the proper spirit
of celebration' (*SC*, 49). The use of a piece
of music that focusses on peace but is not

expressly part of the liturgy can serve to distract from the Agnus Dei which follows.

Why not, instead, sing the Agnus Dei (Lamb of God) to accompany the Breaking of Bread, the Body of Christ, who gave his life so that we could have true peace?

The *GIRM* states, 'It is not permitted to substitute other chants for those found in the Order of Mass, such as the Agnus Dei [Lamb of God]' (366). It has become a common practice for the Lamb of God to be replaced with a piece sung during the sign of peace; yet, this is meant as preparation for the reception of communion rather than as a rite on its own.

Why not bring back the singing of the Lamb of God instead of another piece, as a reminder of the one who calls us into peace

in the first place, the one to whom we pray
'Grant us peace'?

Some composers combine the Lamb of
God with the Communion Hymn to show
the unity between the Fraction and the
faithful's reception of the Eucharist. Some
examples of this are Tom Kendzia's 'Taste
and See' and Ian Callanan's 'Come Feast
at This Table'. The melody begins with
the threefold Lamb of God and then is
continually played while the priest says:
'Behold the Lamb of God …' The hymn
then continues with 'taste and see' or 'come
feast at this table', calling the community to
do just that.

Why not try this approach during the
Communion Rite to connect what is taken,
blessed and broken with what is given to

those who participate in the eucharistic celebration?

While the Priest is receiving the Sacrament, the Communion Chant is begun. Its purpose being to express the communicants' union in spirit by means of the unity of their voices ... and to highlight more clearly the 'communitarian' nature of the procession to receive Communion. (GIRM, 86)

Why not take this on board and begin the Communion Hymn (or chant) while the priest is receiving, so as to highlight the integral connection in the Communion Rite between the breaking of the eucharistic bread and the procession of the communicants to receive it? This also strongly emphasises that the music chosen for this time should be expressive of the ritual action that is taking place.

The movement of the congregation to the altar to receive communion is to be seen as a procession.

Why not ensure that the music sung at this time involves a refrain like 'Stay with us Lord (we pray you)' (*The Veritas Hymnal*) or 'Gifts of Finest Wheat' (*Alleluia Amen*), so that those proceeding to the altar don't need to carry a hymn sheet but are able to remember and sing a response that will help them prepare to receive the Eucharist?

Our celebration of the Eucharist is made up of various rites that, over time, have been amalgamated into the liturgy we now celebrate. It might seem a small thing, but the prayer after communion is just that; it ends the rite of communion as it prays for the fruits of the mystery just celebrated. It is not the concluding prayer of the Mass.

Why not ensure that any elements that are not an integral part of the rite of communion (announcements, thank yous, etc.) are reserved until after the prayer is recited, so that it may truly fulfil its purpose?

The option to clean the vessels for the Eucharist at another table is given.

Why not take this option, at Sunday Eucharist especially? This allows the altar to be cleared of vessels that are not necessary.

Chapter Five

Vessels and Space

Church decor should contribute toward
the church's noble simplicity rather than
ostentation. In the choice of materials for church
appointments there should be a concern for
genuineness of materials and an intent to foster
the instruction of the faithful and the dignity of
the entire sacred place. (GIRM, 292)

The sense of the sacred in liturgy is
enhanced by the various elements that are
used, whether they are vessel, vestment or
book. Their worthiness for the liturgy is
not dependent upon any ornate or elaborate
design but their texture, form and colour.

Why not ask if all that we use in our
celebrations is of noble simplicity? This
is a long-standing principle in the liturgy.
Simplicity does not mean cheap or tatty but

that the essence of each object, no matter how functional, would be worthy of its task.

It is said that cleanliness is next to godliness. Before we come to the end of the liturgical year why not take the opportunity to have the sacred vessels used in the liturgy (chalice, ciborium and patens) properly cleaned? Overuse can tarnish the materials to give a sense of faded beauty.

Why not, for hygiene reasons, and for the sake of reverence, have all sacred vessels sparkling before the new year begins?

'Liturgy happens not just within the sanctuary but throughout the whole sacred space.' The primary elements of the sanctuary are: altar, ambo, chair, cross and, in some cases, tabernacle. Anything else can detract from these essential items.

Why not try to find other suitable places in the church to introduce areas that focus on particular themes, devotions or seasonal expressions that may be a custom in certain communities? In so doing, we are able to use the whole church in a more appropriate manner.

October is the month of the Rosary and the Missions. It can be one of those times when there is an uneasy tension between the role of the church as a place to celebrate the sacraments and as a place for devotional and private prayer. Within the place of worship, the liturgy should be central, but the faithful are led to a deeper participation by those things that may be introduced to aid devotion. The primary example of this is the Stations of the Cross. They are placed along a processional route within the church, distinct from the sanctuary, that leads those who meditate upon them towards the altar.

Why not ensure this principle is kept for all other elements of devotion, so as to leave the place of celebration uncluttered but the devotions of the faithful respected?

Liturgy is a living thing, but the enthusiasm for Easter decorations can become faded as the season moves on, especially if flowers are wilting around the paschal candle or baptismal font.

Why not ensure that any temporary decorations that we use, like flowers, speak the right theology and are what they are meant to be – something that is alive? Each

of these elements needs to be at the service
of what the liturgy as a whole is trying to
express.

A lot of attention in liturgy can be focussed
on the sanctuary area and those who
minister there. The assembly, however, also
have an integral role in the celebration and
their place also needs to serve the function
they hold. Their benches or chairs, the
GIRM mentions, should be arranged in such
a way that the people can easily take up the
postures required for the different parts
of the celebration, and that they can easily
come forward to receive holy communion.

Why not assess the arrangement and
spacing of seating and the ability of the
worshipping community to, without
hindrance, move through the church or

worship space, so that all may have full, conscious and active participation?

The Stations of the Cross form an important part of the devotions of the Season of Lent. In St Mel's Cathedral in Longford there is a collection of sculptures depicting each of the stations by the artist Ken Thompson that brings the story vividly to life.

Why not take time to visit or look up these stations during this Season of Lent to draw inspiration for how you can develop them in your own parish?

In many cathedrals and churches an ambry can be found. It holds the holy oils and sacred chrism, which have been blessed at the Chrism Mass of Holy Week. However, it can sometimes be difficult for people who view these to distinguish between them.

Why not use vessels that, while they may complement each other, also vary in colour or design, so as to draw attention to the difference between each of these oils and highlight the distinctive function and purpose they hold?

'Floral decorations should always be done with moderation' (*GIRM*, 305). If they are in harmony with the liturgical season and the liturgical setting, they can add greatly to the celebration. The reverse is also true: flowers and decorations not in keeping with season and setting will greatly detract from the liturgy.

Why not ensure that all the floral decorations we use in church are genuine and fresh so as to reflect a liturgy that is alive and not artificial?

From time to time we need to do a good spring clean. Clutter can build up quickly in any setting and our churches are not immune. The sanctuary especially can end up full of extras that are not needed. Essentially, the sanctuary is the place of the altar, ambo and chair.

Why not ensure that only those things that are necessary remain so that their symbolism is clearer? Remember that sometimes less is more!

The attention we pay to the liturgy expresses the significance of the elements that are used in it. We would never think of cluttering the tabernacle with other items and yet the altar table, and ambo, can in some churches become storage facilities for notices, old books, or items that are just being hidden from public view.

Why not ensure that these are kept clear of all unessential items and that the key items associated with them may be clearly seen: the Bread and Wine on the altar, and the Word of God alone on the ambo?

The altar table is the heart of any church and yet its sacredness can be diminished by wires or microphone plugs fixed to it.

Why not ensure that these are fitted to the floor and not to the altar table itself?

The books used for the liturgy should be 'worthy, dignified and beautiful', because they serve as signs and symbols of heavenly realities (*GIRM*, 349). The instruction also uses the word 'veneration' in respect of the Book of the Gospels and lectionaries.

Why not ensure that these are stored carefully in a special place when not being used in the liturgy, so as to preserve their good condition and respect the dignity of the Word of God?

All that we use for the liturgy is to be noble, worthy and beautiful. These elements should be exclusive to the liturgy. We can be tempted to use modern technology like laptops or iPhones for the liturgy if away from home. These, however, do not fulfil the requirements of the *GIRM*.

Why not ensure that when travelling you always use a missal or lectionary that is worthy of the liturgy being celebrated?

Chapter Six

Throughout the Year

During the course of the year, the mysteries of redemption are recalled so as in some way to be made present. (*GIRM*, 16)

The seasons can be a time when we put effort into decorating our churches. However, it is important to remember that whatever is added for a temporary period should not detract from the elements of the church that are central, namely the altar, ambo, chair (*GIRM*, 296–310).

Why not ensure that, in that spirit, any decoration of the altar, which should be restricted, would be placed around the altar, and not upon it? Only those elements that are needed are to be placed there: the Book of the Gospels and the sacred vessels.

We have all been commenting on the abandonment of the Season of Advent to Christmas commercialism. But we are also noticing that the Season of Christmas is becoming a thing of the past as well. Once Christmas Day is over, there seems to be little enthusiasm for Epiphany, Baptism of Our Lord – and definitely not for the Presentation of Our Lord.

Why not use these times and the Sundays of January as signs of 'Christ with us', express them as what they are – manifestations – and make it a 'Season of Christ's presence with us'?

It is a constant battle to keep the spirit of Advent alive with the sounds and smells of Christmas all around.

Why not keep to one psalm response during the Sundays of Advent, for example 'Maranatha, Come Lord Jesus'? This would remind us of what we are celebrating in Advent, acting like a mantra through its repetition. It could become a constant prayer, filling our lives during the season. It could also be used as a gospel acclamation and as a response to the Prayer of the Faithful.

Advent is a time of anticipation, waiting and hope. It has a character that is distinct from the Season of Lent.

Why not distinguish between these two seasons by using different shades of purple? If blue-purple is used in Advent and violet in Lent, the character of each season is respected and proclaimed. Reflecting the season's colour in church decoration as well as in the vestments worn can also help to achieve this.

Advent and Christmas have been filled with elements that, while not fundamental, have become very much part of the liturgy of these seasons: Advent wreath, Christmas tree, crib, carol service. One of the most ancient traditions at this time has been The Great O's, the Magnificat Antiphons sung or recited from 17 to 24 December.

Why not use these texts throughout this period as the basis of the music for the liturgies, decorations on banners, Christmas tree or the church itself, as well as for the scripture at carol services? They will provide a deeper understanding of the wonder of the Incarnation that we celebrate at this time.

Sometimes you hear people say Christmas is only for children; perhaps because the reality is that this period of the year can be a time that is difficult or lonely for many.

Why not make our churches, from Advent to Christmas to Epiphany, places where people can take refuge from their anxieties and loneliness? Not just during our liturgies but also throughout these seasons, let our churches be spaces where, through their warmth, beauty and atmosphere, the faithful can find Emmanuel, God with us.

Much like the Feast of Pentecost, which liturgically seems to be forgotten about the next day, the Feast of the Epiphany often seems to be over before it has started. This feast, however, is more than just the coming of the Magi; its focus is the Manifestation of the Lord. Look at the antiphon for evening prayer, which mentions Magi, Cana and Baptism.

Why not keep that spirit of 'Revealing Christ to the Nations' alive throughout the month of January and have it as a way of bringing together and expressing the other elements that have developed in that period, such as World Day of Migrants and Refugees, Week of Prayer for Christian Unity and Catholic Schools Week?

There are a certain number of ancient feasts that, when they coincide with a Sunday in Ordinary Time, take precedence. The Feast of the Presentation is one of these and it takes the place of a Sunday this year.

Why not use this opportunity, with the larger Sunday assembly, to develop the custom of a procession on this feast before the Eucharist, somewhat like Palm Sunday, with the blessing and lighting of candles? It will help to link the Feast of Christmas with the springtime of the year and the belief that Jesus is the light of the world, which this feast expresses.

The Eucharist rightly plays a vital role at the heart of the life of the Church. Faith in the Eucharist cannot be presumed but must, instead, be fostered. The period between Lent and Easter gives us a wonderful opportunity to do just that, as we come to celebrate Holy Thursday especially and later on Corpus Christi.

Why not use this period to prepare, and make available, material in newsletters or as part of homilies to help the faithful come to a deeper understanding of the Eucharist – the source and summit of the Christian life?

Lent is a good time to develop different aspects of our celebration of the liturgy. The new translation of the Missal includes aspects that are new to us for Lent as well, such as the addition of a prayer over the people for each day of the season. The removal of the Gloria from the Gathering Rite is another changed aspect and calls on us to reflect on the way we carry it out.

Why not look at the alternative penitential act – 'Have mercy on us, O Lord' – which in the older missal seemed to be rarely used? Bernard Sexton in his setting of this, found in *Sing the Mass*, gives a useful tone that shows very effectively how, through music, a dialogue can be developed between celebrant, choir and assembly. This expresses well the unique role that each has within the liturgy.

Sometimes less is more; this is very true in our churches during the Season of Lent. The custom of emptying the church of flowers and decoration draws our attention to the discipline and restraint of this period.

Why not reintroduce this tradition of restraint for the season and ensure that all who come into the church over these weeks come to know that this is a time apart? In turn, the joy of Easter can then be better expressed and the glimpse at Laetare will make greater sense. This is true for our music as well – remember no 'Alleluias'.

Lent is a time when we anticipate Good Friday with the practice of celebrating the Stations of the Cross, but it is also the time of anticipating the Easter Vigil in the preparatory Rite of Christian Initiation of Adults, which is closely linked with this season.

Why not highlight this in the liturgy during Lent by using aspects of the rite on the various Sundays of Lent? Even if the parish has no candidates for the RCIA programme, there are many parishes that have and we all would benefit from the period of purification and enlightenment that it offers. Not only does Lent prepare for Baptism, but also calls us to reflect on what it means to be a member of the baptised.

The gestures and posture of the priest, the deacon, and the ministers, as well as those of the

people, ought to contribute to making the entire celebration resplendent with beauty and noble simplicity, so that the true and full meaning of the different parts of the celebration is evident and that the participation of all is fostered. (*GIRM*, 42)

Why not use this Season of Lent to begin the good practice of posture as laid out in the *GIRM*: stand from beginning until Collect, Gospel, Preface, Communion Rite, Prayer after Communion and Dismissal; kneel from Sanctus to Doxology, and sit for readings? These postures in themselves are a communal form of prayer, and help to unite the assembly in their work of praise.

In the Season of Lent, emphasis is placed on the sacrament of reconciliation.

Why not prepare for this in one way by ensuring that the place used for the sacrament, whether box or room, is dignified and expressive of the mercy that is administered there and also in keeping with the best practice of safeguarding with a fixed screen?

Often we celebrate our feasts and seasons as boxes to be ticked rather than opportunities to encounter the paschal mystery.

Why not emphasise the unity of Holy Week from Palm Sunday to Easter by encouraging the Stations of the Cross, offering meditations on the passion at Masses during the week, or preparing a meditation space in a suitable place in the church that highlights the passion, death and Resurrection of our Lord, so as to enable the faithful to experience a deeper expression of this week as the core of our faith?

The Easter Triduum is a unique celebration and highlight of the liturgical year. While we might be inclined to see this as three separate ceremonies, it is in essence only one, celebrated over three days, from the beginning of the Lord's Supper to the conclusion of the Easter Vigil.

Why not try to emphasise this by maintaining an atmosphere in the church over the period that highlights it as a sacred time above all others? This would mean that, in the silence and stillness of those days, even outside of the formal liturgies themselves we can be drawn closer to the paschal mystery that they express.

Easter begins with the lighting of the paschal candle. It is honoured with incense and the proclamation of the Exsultet. It has formed part of the Easter Liturgy since the fifth century. After Pentecost it is returned to the area of Baptism but can be by this time in a sorry state, with dead flowers and melted wax still fixed to it.

Why not ensure that it is always well maintained so that it can clearly speak of the symbolism that it is meant to suggest?

'Alleluia' is the liturgical word that we use so frequently during the Easter Season.

Why not also sing it at every Mass during the rest of the year (except Lent)? The people will need no words to follow, but can just join in. It is a useful way of encouraging congregations to sing and a way of encouraging those that might have remained silent before. Just use the same setting each day, maybe for a season, until it is well established. Singing is the best way to get everybody to participate; no matter what part of the church they may be in they can equally take part when they sing. The 'Amen' is another good place to start.

The *Directory on Popular Piety and the Liturgy* (*DPPL*) tells of the Pentecost Novena (155). This novena begins on the Feast of the Ascension as a time of awaiting, being 'clothed with the power from on high' (Lk 24:49). In some places this is used as a period of prayer for Christian unity – we have only to think of the disciples and Mary gathered together in the same place when the Spirit came.

Why not use this time as a period of coming together with other Christians in your area and plan events, including liturgies, to increase our desire for the fulfilment of those words of our Lord, 'May they all be one'?

The Feast of the Body and Blood of Christ is marked in many places with Corpus Christi processions. They not only give devotion to the Blessed Sacrament, but are also a sign of the Body of Christ, the Church communities in each local area. This is echoed each time we celebrate the Eucharist. The communion procession symbolises the Body receiving the Body, the Bride going to meet the Bridegroom, the pilgrim Church on its way to the Kingdom.

Why not ensure that this procession is not just functional but also dignified and carried out in a reverential way, accompanied by appropriate music to highlight this symbol of communion?

June sees the celebration of the feast days of a number of Irish saints. With the new translation of the Missal, work has been done on the prayers for these local saints' days.

Why not add these to the parish liturgical resources as a way to develop these memorials and their significance to us now?

October is the month of the Rosary. The *DPPL* tells us that Marian devotions should have, in varying degrees, a Trinitarian expression that characterises God revealed in the New Testament, as well as constant recourse to Sacred Scripture as it relates to the particular season (186–7). The liturgy presents us with such an opportunity in the memorials of the Blessed Virgin Mary on Saturdays. The *DPPL* goes on to say that the ancient custom of remembering the maternal example and discipleship of Mary is a prelude to the Sunday memorial of the Lord's Resurrection. Mary was the disciple who kept vigil on that first Holy Saturday in expectation of the Lord's rising.

Why not use the Saturday celebration as a good way of fostering a link between the liturgy and devotion during this month?

Summorum Pontificum, Pope Benedict's *motu proprio* on the use of the older missal of 1962, has at its heart the heritage we find in the liturgy and the constant need for reverence. Gregorian chant has a very

special place in the heart of the Church
because of its heritage and the reverence it
brings to our celebrations.

Why not, in the month of November
when we think of the faithful departed,
reintroduce some parts of the Requiem
Mass, for example the Sanctus or Agnus
Dei? These chants have a significant part
to play in the liturgy, whether celebrated in
the ordinary or extraordinary rite.

CHAPTER SEVEN

Sacraments and Sacramentals

Every event in life to be sanctified by divine grace that flows from the paschal mystery. (***GIRM**, 368*)

Baptism is highlighted as an important aspect of the Easter Season and takes a significant part in our liturgical celebrations at this time. Sometimes the baptistery can end up being used as a place to store chairs, tables and other items not in use. The Book of Blessings tells us, 'A baptistery ... is to be set aside exclusively for Baptism as befits the place where, from the womb of the Church, so to speak, Christians are reborn through water and the Holy Spirit.'

Why not try to find other places for storage so as to preserve the dignity the baptistery rightly deserves?

Weddings are popular in the summer months. Sometimes people feel obliged to follow the customs that have developed around the time of marriage. The tradition of the bride being given away by her father, for example, need not necessarily be adhered to. The rite of marriage states, 'If there is a procession to the altar, the ministers go first, followed by the priest, and then the bride and bridegroom. According to local custom, they may be escorted by at least their parents and the two witnesses.'

Why not explore with the couple the various options instead of feeling that tradition always has to be followed?

During the summer months, and in the period leading up to the summer months, many couples will be meeting members of parish teams to plan their weddings.

Why not ensure that there is plenty of material, not just for the legal or theological elements, but also the liturgical aspects, so as to help prepare the liturgy? These should include not just the suitable scriptures but also the musical and decoration guidelines and an overview of what we understand the marriage ceremony to mean. It is important that we provide every resource to show the wonderful and enriching possibilities that are available, which can express both the Church's understanding of the sacrament and the specific desires of each bride and groom.

We have a tendency to privatise the celebration of the sacraments. People often feel uncomfortable going into the church if there is a Baptism or wedding taking place, and yet these are celebrations of the whole parish. By its very nature, the sacrament of the sick, the celebration of 'commending those who are ill to the suffering and glorified Lord', most often takes place with only a few people. When conditions permit, however, it may be a part of the celebration of the Eucharist.

Why not from time to time hold this celebration in the church or another suitable place, such as a hospital or nursing home, so that those who are seriously ill or those weakened by old age may avail of the sacrament as a community? Those who attend but are not seriously ill can still be invited to come forward for a blessing, similar to those who do not receive the Eucharist at Mass.

November is the month in which we commemorate the faithful departed. It is also an opportunity to reflect on the way we celebrate the funeral rites of those who have died.

Why not read once again the introduction to these rites during this month? Or learn some new liturgical music that would be appropriate and that would be the bearer of meaning and consolation to those who mourn?

The Introductory Rites 'have the character of a beginning, introduction and preparation' (*GIRM*, 46). In certain celebrations, like the reception of the remains before a funeral, they are omitted or take place in a particular way.

Why not be aware of this and in a particular way at funerals use it as the period to gather symbols or have the personal reflection on the deceased given, so that the Collect and the celebration of the Eucharist can flow out of this as the Christian response to our understanding of death?

Funerals are community events where the whole community gathers to support the bereaved and pray for those who have died. Quite often, however, that sense of community can be difficult to achieve in the liturgy, as the people who gather to take part in it come from diverse places and, therefore, the way they participate in the liturgy may vary greatly.

Why not begin to sing 'Song of Farewell' from the ritual book at all funerals in the parish as a way to unite the assembly? It is accessible and easy to take up for all assemblies, even the most reluctant ones, and it helps all to take a greater part in the liturgy.

The funeral of a loved one is extremely difficult for a family, and there can be an added pressure if there is the expectation that they must read or lead the prayers.

Why not develop the option, as some parishes do, of having funeral support teams that are able to lead the readings or prayers for a family, so that the family are ministered to as well during the liturgy?

CHAPTER EIGHT

How We Are Shaped by Sacred Space

Church architecture is something I have always been fascinated by. It has been my good fortune to have been involved over the last number of years with two major church renovations: The Church of St Mary of the Assumption, Carrick-on-Shannon, County Leitrim; and the Cathedral of St Mel, County Longford. In both of these the architect Richard Hurley was involved and from him I gained a great appreciation of how a space shapes us and influences us in worship.

Before either of these renovations Richard had worked on the Augustinian church in Galway City. This work transformed not only the church but also the way the community there celebrates the liturgy. While on holidays in Galway once, I joined in the celebration of the Sunday

Eucharist there and was greatly impressed by the ownership the community had of the liturgy and their appreciation of the liturgy as something alive and active. What impressed me most of all was that two people from the community, seeing that I was new, came over to welcome me. It was something that became possible because of the antiphonal way the church was laid out, allowing people to notice each other as a community.

After the Second Vatican Council many churches were reordered, some in ways that caused great pain to the local community and in some ways that might have been trying too hard to make a point about a new way of worship. You can never force a space to be what it is not. Any reordering of a church needs to be sensitive to its environment. You need to understand the dynamics of a space before you can let the liturgy be alive in it. The liturgy must be in continuity with the past, not a break from it.

The first concern must be what the axis of the building is and how to utilise it. The place has to be found where the altar can naturally be anchored because all else – ambo, assembly, chair, tabernacle – will relate to it. Remember that the sanctuary is not a stage but the heart of the whole worship space, which begins once you enter.

To walk through the door of any church is to enter into a particular kind of space. Through the ages many have created, developed and redeveloped ways in which the mystery of our faith can be suggested and symbolised by design and decoration; however, this is something that needs to be authentic and not contrived. In a sense, the church building can become a sign and symbol of the faith itself.

This idea is best expressed through the analysis of specific church buildings and the liturgy that surrounds them. By way of example, I offer an overview of the Rite of Dedication of St Mel's Cathedral below. The symbolism of this liturgy is expressive not simply of the completion of a renovation after the fire that destroyed it on Christmas Day in 2009 but of the power of what the liturgy can achieve in conveying who and what we are as a worshipping community in a particular time and place.

Following this we take a walk through St Mary's Church in Carrick-on-Shannon after its renovation. It is in seeing the significance that each element holds, even those elements that could be perceived as insignificant, that we begin to read the building as a text of the mystery of our faith; the visible architecture opening our eyes to the invisible.

Who and what we are

The reopening of St Mel's Cathedral has had an immense effect not only on the local community but also on the large number of people who come to visit the cathedral. The competency, skill and insightfulness of many have created a structure that is faithful to the past, while also building for the future.

Many events took place to mark this most historic event for Longford and the diocese of Ardagh and Clonmacnois. At the heart of all of these was the dedication on 17 May 2015. The Rite of Dedication of a church is so much more than the blessing or official opening of a building; it is an acknowledgement of who and what we are as a Christian community who come to use it. The word most commonly used for a Christian place of worship is 'church', and that is first and foremost the name of the community itself (*ecclesia*). In the case of a cathedral, the name comes from the chair of the bishop (*cathedra*). In other words, it is the place that expresses the relationship between the faithful of the diocese and the bishop appointed to shepherd, administer and teach the gospel to the Christian community. The Rite of Dedication takes as its heart this relationship. It begins with expressing the faith of the Christian community and dedicating this holy place to reflect those who gather.

In the case of St Mel's this liturgy is being called a re-dedication, to highlight the connection with the community who have gathered on this site down the years, both in the pre-fire cathedral and the church before it. It is also called the dedication of the altar, because the altar lies at the heart of each church, as Christ lies at the heart of each community. The altar makes the church what it is.

The Rite of Dedication is by its nature an extraordinary event. It is never a commonplace celebration, as it only takes place once at the beginning of the lifetime of a church, or, as in the case of St Mel's, after a major alteration. This is because the rite is an initiation, like the way a Christian is initiated into the Church. The nature of this is not as a rite of passage but a *becoming* in our life. A church becomes a church as a Christian becomes a Christian, through Baptism, Confirmation and Eucharist. The rite begins with a washing with water, an anointing of oil and a celebration of the Eucharist. This in itself reminds us of the innate link between the building and its community; they can never be separated from each other.

The first movement of the rite for St Mel's begins with the opening of the cathedral doors. In itself a practical element but symbolically it is to express that this is a place open for all who are searching for the Lord in their lives. The words used reflect how we do that: 'May we open our hearts and minds to receive his word with faith; may our fellowship, born in the one font of Baptism and sustained at the one table of the Lord, become the one temple of his Spirit.' There is an old tradition that as the bishop crosses the threshold of the church for the first time, he carries the

Book of the Gospels; how fitting this is, because central to the role of the bishop is the shepherding of the whole people of God by proclaiming the gospel and sharing it in their lives. A bishop's first act is to reverence a crucifix that is presented to him by the community to remind him of the welcome they give him to share the teachings of the faith.

The procession then moves to the sanctuary, but the altar is not venerated as it has yet to be dedicated. The first part of the ritual is the blessing of water. Here again is expressed that ultimate understanding of the Church as community: 'Make it a sign of the saving waters of Baptism, by which we become one in Christ, the temple of your Spirit.' It is first sprinkled on the people and then on the walls. Our entrance into the cathedral is now constantly a reminder of *who we are* as the baptised faithful. The font marks the beginning of everything for us as Christians. It is the doorway through which we enter the life of faith. It marks the axis that leads us on our journey to the altar and the sustaining power of the Lord.

Once the Liturgy of the Word is celebrated the Rite of Dedication of the altar begins. First of all there is an invitation to prayer because who does the dedicating? The entire Christian community united with the communion of saints in heaven. And so the litany is sung reminding us of the community of those who have gone before us to their place in heaven and continue to intercede for us as the pilgrim Church on earth. From the early days of the Church there has been a tradition of placing the relics of the saints in the altar as a reminder of the link with the Church in heaven. The nature of the altar in St Mel's necessitated that this take place before the altar was installed and so the Rite of Dedication had been an ongoing ritual since the first day the altar arrived in the cathedral.

The bishop then leads the Prayer of Dedication, which continues to express the mystery of the Church with the imagery of the bride of Christ, the chosen vineyard, the dwelling place of God on earth, a beacon to the whole world.

The anointing of the altar brings out clearly what the altar is meant to be: the symbol of Christ's presence among us. The word 'Christ' means 'anointed one'. The altar here leaves us in no doubt as to what it is: the rock who is Christ, the ever stable and certain presence of the Lord and the sign of the Lord in the midst of his people, the head of the body, the Church. The whole *mensa* or top of the altar is anointed with the fragrant oil of chrism. This oil was consecrated at the Chrism Mass on Holy Thursday. It reflects the presence of the Lord administered to the faithful through the sacraments. Following this the walls are also anointed in twelve places. This is a clear allusion to the twelve apostles who are expressed in the liturgy as the pillars of the faith, and so of the Church as a whole: 'The walls of the city had twelve courses of stone as its foundation, on which were written the names of the twelve apostles of the Lamb' (Rv 21:14).

The incensation of the altar and the church follows this with the placing of a brazier on the altar and the building being filled with the fragrance of its scent. The fragrance acceptable to the Father is that which comes from Christ's Easter sacrifice, as we read in St Paul: 'Follow the way of love, even as Christ loves you. He gave himself for us as an offering to God, a gift of pleasing fragrance' (Eph 5:2). The Book of Revelation says that incense is also a symbol of prayer that rises to God. The assembled faithful are incensed as well as the altar and building to remind us that the temple of God where we are to offer spiritual worship is the individual baptised Christian and at the same time the whole assembly. The first to be incensed after the altar is the bishop at his *cathedra* as a sign of his role and calling to sanctify the people of God.

The preparation of the altar for the Eucharist begins with the lighting of the altar candles. These are not on the altar but next to it, so as to highlight the significance of the altar itself. The altar is the place for the bread and wine, these humble gifts that we offer from our lives, but by the grace of God become for us the Body and Blood of Christ. The candles always remind us that Christ is the light of the world, a light that no darkness can overcome, the light that comes to be truly present for us at the altar of the Eucharist. These are also lit over the places on the walls that have been anointed with holy chrism.

The altar is dressed for the celebration like a newly baptised Christian. The white garment reflects the purity of life we find in Christ and the sign of Resurrection that the white cloth stood for in the empty tomb of the first Easter day. The Eucharist is celebrated as the final act of this Rite of Dedication. It is the source and summit of all the activity of the Church, for the Church is never more itself than when it is gathered to celebrate the Eucharist. From here the strength is found for the Church to be the bread of life for all in the world.

While the Rite of Dedication only happens once, the celebration of the Eucharist will be a constant reminder of *who and what we are as a Christian Community*. The liturgy will end with the dismissal back into the world, back out through the doors that have been opened at the beginning of this liturgy. The final words, *Ite Missa Est*, are symbolic of where the title of the Mass comes from. We gather to be sent out, we gather to be transformed by Christ, we gather to remind ourselves of what we are called to be, Christ's presence alive in the world today.

'Peace to all people of good will': A Walk through St Mary's Church in Carrick-on-Shannon

For those who first developed the Gothic style of architecture honesty was an important element. The building was to be something pared down to the minimum, to just have what was needed. The immense blocks of pillars and the resulting darkened interiors of the Romanesque giving way to the slender columns and walls pierced through with numerous panelled windows illuminating the interiors, simply achieved by the development of the pointed arch. This in itself lifted the eyes heavenward and highlighted the goal of the builders of these places to raise our minds and hearts to God. Throughout mainland Europe during the Middle Ages and beyond this style flourished. One of the greatest examples of this has to be Notre-Dame, Paris. Here the style grew not just into a cathedral but also a place of pilgrimage. In the nineteenth century the revival of this style of architecture coincided with many great Irish churches being built after Catholic Emancipation. A typical example of this is St Mary's in Carrick-on-Shannon and it is with the themes of honesty and pilgrimage in mind that we analyse the structural elements of St Mary's.

Approaching the entrance from the street front, the relief sculpturing over the doorway introduces the patronage of the Church: Our Lady of the Assumption. Reflecting this devotion, Mary appears in many forms, both within the church and in the grounds outside. The title St Mary Major was associated with the church in earlier years. It is Mary who welcomes us inside. Entering the double doors, we see another old title for many churches: *Domus Dei, Porta Coeli* (House of God, Gateway to Heaven). As we stand within its walls, the psalm comes to mind, 'And now our feet

are standing in your gateways, Jerusalem'
(Ps 122:2).

Coming through the three entrance
archways brings up the point of honesty,
each element is not just decorative but
suggestive in a symbolic way of our faith
and the way we worship. These arches
express both Father, Son and Spirit, and the
characteristics of Christ as priest, prophet
and king. Maybe they could challenge us to
see ourselves as, in the words of 1 Peter 2:9,
a 'royal priesthood, a holy nation, a people
set apart'.

Symbolic language is not something that
is fixed to one interpretation but evolves
with the viewer over time.

One definite symbol that strikes each
person is the position of the baptismal font,
at the start of the axis that leads to the
altar. Here we all as Christians begin our
pilgrim way. Standing next to the font, we
can see two windows to the left depicting
the Baptism of Our Lord in the Jordan but

also next to it we see the Agony in the Garden. In a sense, this awakens us to the reality that when we are baptised we enter the tomb with Christ. The font becomes the foot of the cross on Calvary. We take the place of St John and think of Mary who welcomed us here, and we hear the words of her son once more, 'Behold your Mother, Behold your Child.' As we bless ourselves with that water of Baptism, we embrace our total selves with the sign of the cross now drawn as we are to the altar.

The altar speaks of Christ for it is the centre of this worship space. All eyes are drawn to it. It marks the place of Christ's body on the cross, with arms outstretched to ambo and chair like the extended hands of Jesus as he preached the gospel and healed the sick. Where it stands marks the head of the nave, a word whose origins are in *navis*, Latin word for 'ship'. Christ stands at the head of our boat; and, like the storm at sea, we come scared by the turmoil of life.

In our encounter with Christ, he commands us to 'be still, be calm', and so it is.

We are in the place of God encompassed by twelve pillars: twelve tribes of Israel; twelve pillars of the temple in Jerusalem; twelve apostles; twelve baskets left from the multiplication of loaves and fishes. Above witness the saints who have gone before us, unnamed and unknown, women and men, they stand for all who have gone before us marked with the sign of faith and join us in our worship of God.

We are standing in the sanctuary of God. This is the place of encounter between heaven and earth; around in the plasterwork there are angels with symbols of the Eucharist, with wheat and vine, as well as the passion, with nails and crown of thorns. For as we gather around the altar as those of the early Church did we stand equal in God's presence. The square shape of the altar is a symbol of the world; it is surrounded by the circular disc that

rises to the back as a symbol of the eternal.
Held between the two of these is the real
presence preserved in the tabernacle calling
us to believe that we stand on holy ground.

Above in the stained-glass window is the
cross, the altar of Christ's sacrifice, standing
between Incarnation and Resurrection,
the mysteries that give us our identity
and destiny as Christians. This series of
windows tells us in pictorial form the words
of St Paul: 'Though he was in the form of
God, Jesus did not count equality with God
a thing to be grasped. He emptied himself
taking the form of a servant, being born
into human likeness, and yet humbler yet
even to accepting death, death on a cross
but God raised him high and gave him the
name which is above all names.'

And so while we stand here at Calvary,
our minds are raised to see that this is
also the empty tomb, that Christ who was
sacrificed has indeed risen from the dead,
and calls each one into a relationship with

him. Our journey does not end here but calls us to a deeper discovery. Through the sacristy a new adoration room can be found; reminiscent of an early monastic chapel, it offers a place of peace and calm to delve into the depths of the mystery that we celebrate in our worship.

Returning to the main part of the church, angels on either side hold up a phrase from the Gloria: 'Peace to all people of good will.' As that wish is offered to us we walk back down through the church. A new window to the right speaks in many ways: some see the pierced side of Christ; others life-giving water flowing from the side of the temple.

With eyes raised over the entrance, we see the gallery window, showing some of the symbols relating to Mary from the Litany of the Blessed Virgin. Over this, angels with censors lead to the image of Christ the King, an image common to many early European Gothic churches, the abiding image for the pilgrim as they return to the world.

We go out to announce the Good News. The arches that welcomed us in become those of faith, hope and love as we go out: faith with the Book of the Gospels; hope with the paschal candle; and love with the holy oils. As we open the door to return to the outside, we take with us something of the experience we have just had.

Sing psalms and hymns and inspired songs to
God and never cease in giving him thanks.

(Eph 5:19)

This pattern of prayer is what we ourselves
have gathered to take part in, at this hour.

We are told also: 'For although you have
no need of our praise, yet our thanksgiving
is itself your gift, since our praises do not
add to your greatness but profit us for
salvation.'

So what we do here is also for our good,
it brings us to another place, it broadens our
view of how God has worked in the world,
it puts into our mouths the words of those
who have over the years seen that presence
of God continue to be alive. It gives us a
way to give our thanks for the good things
we have been given today.

For when we do so we come to see
beyond ourselves and the concerns of our
life.

It echoes the eternal answers that our faith has to offer, so that we can learn to take for ourselves those words that Mary and so many others have used before: 'My soul proclaims the greatness of the Lord and my spirit exalts in God my saviour.'